I0816204

TABLE OF CONTENTS

A Pelican Book

Teaching Tips for Caregivers and Teachers:

Research shows that one of the best ways for students to learn a new topic is to read about it.

Before Reading

- Read the title and predict what the book will be about.
- Read the "Words to Know" and discuss the meaning of each word.
- Read the back cover to see what the book is about.

During Reading

- When a student gets to a word that is unknown, ask them to look at the rest of the sentence to find clues to help with the meaning of the unknown word.
- Motivate students with praise and encouragement.

After Reading

- Discuss the main idea of the book.
- Ask students to give one detail that they learned in the book.

Sight Words

all
are
around
by
four
get
go
have
I
most
on
some

Words to Know

car

doors

electric

roads

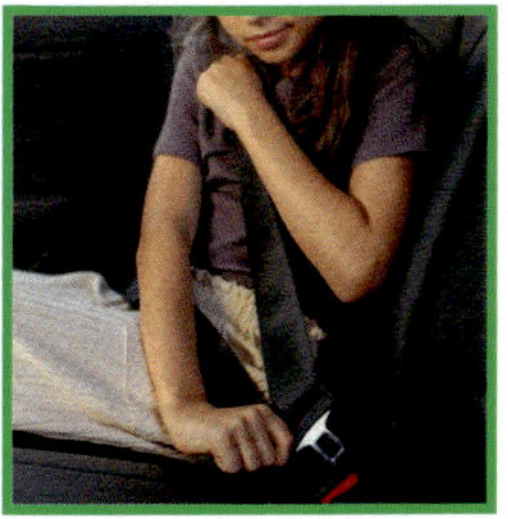
seatbelt

wheels

I get around by **car**.

car
GT R

All cars have
four **wheels**.

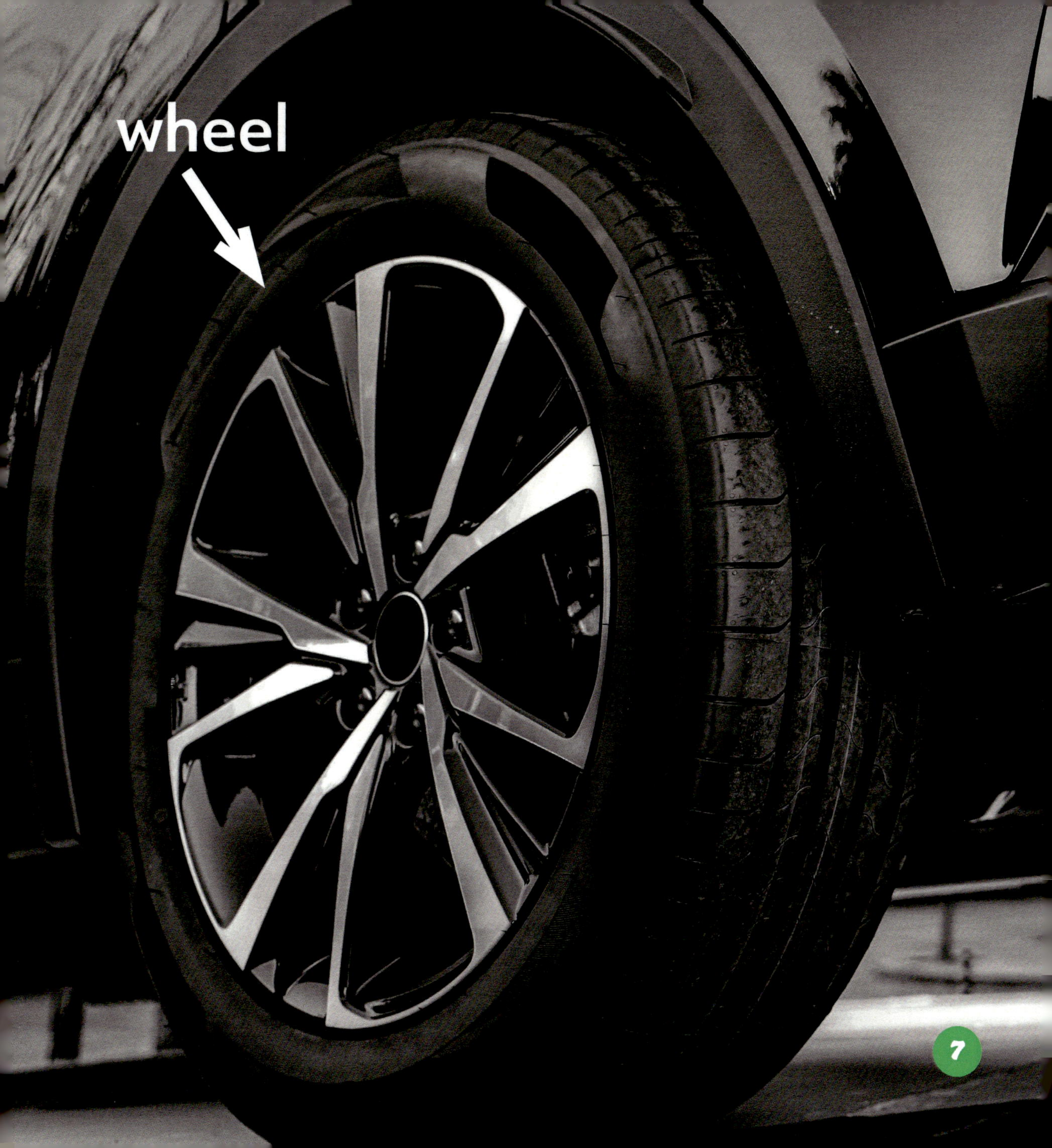
wheel

Most cars have
four **doors**.

door

seatbelt

All cars have **seatbelts**.

Some cars are **electric**.

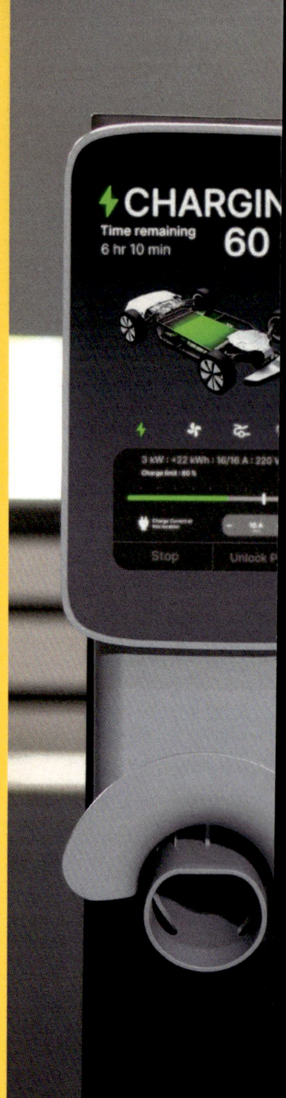

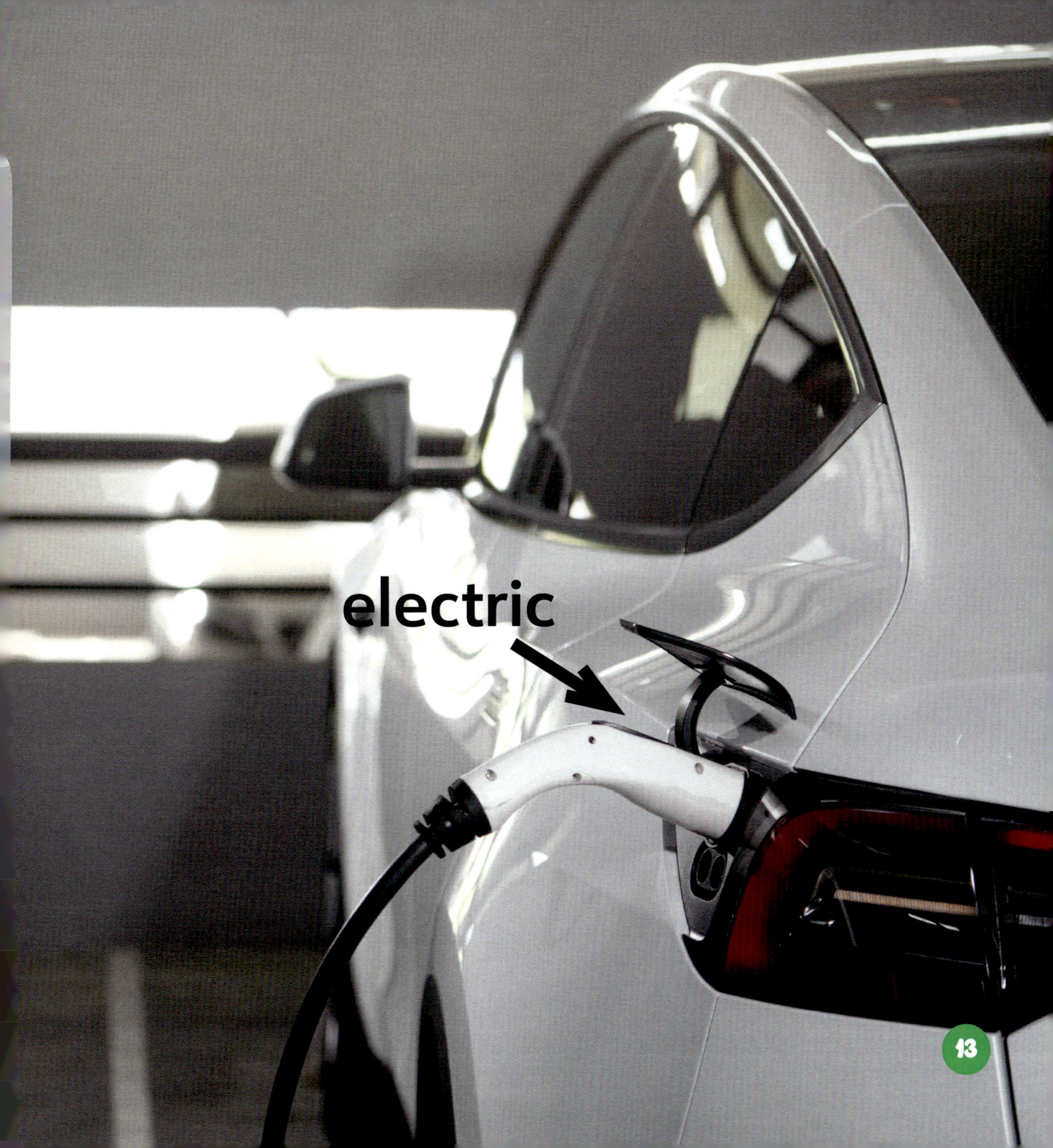
electric

All cars go on **roads**.

road

Index

Written by: Ryan Earley
Design by: Niko Magaro
Editor: Kim Thompson
Series Development: James Earley

Photos: All images from Shutterstock

Library of Congress PCN Data
Cars / Ryan Earley
How I Get Around
ISBN 979-8-8945-9257-2(hard cover)
ISBN 979-8-8945-9271-8(paperback)
ISBN 979-8-8945-9299-2(EPUB)
ISBN 979-8-8945-9285-5(eBook)
ISBN 979-8-8945-9313-5(audio)
ISBN 979-8-8945-9327-2(Read-Along)
Library of Congress Control Number: 2024946360

Printed in Canada/012025/CP20250101

Seahorse Publishing Company
seahorsepub.com

Published in the United States
Seahorse Publishing
PO Box 771325
Coral Springs, FL 33077